Tessitura

Tessitura

Julie Sampson

Shearsman Books

First published in the United Kingdom in 2013 by
Shearsman Books
50 Westons Hill Drive
Emersons Green
BRISTOL BS16 7DF

Shearsman Books Ltd Registered Office
30–31 St. James Place, Mangotsfield, Bristol BS16 9JB
(this address not for correspondence)

www.shearsman.com

ISBN 978-1-84861-239-6

Copyright © Julie Sampson, 2013.

The right of Julie Sampson to be identified as the author
of this work has been asserted by her in accordance with the Copyrights,
Designs and Patents Act of 1988.
All rights reserved.

Acknowledgments

Grateful acknowledgment is made to the editors of these publications in which the following poems have appeared; also to Chrissy Banks, Genista Lewes Mary Maher and the Fire River Poets, for their encouragement and constructive skills. Also, to Bob Mann who introduced me to M.P. Willcocks and her writing; and to staff at Mount Edgcumbe for their assistance with finding Edgcumbe (formerly *Edgecumbe*) family-trees.

Cyclamens and Swords for 'Chervil' and 'That Skeletal Tree'; *Dawntreader* for 'Nuthatch'; *Equinox* for 'Musbury W/rites'; *Exeter Flying Post* for 'Imagining Translation'; 'Margaret Beaufort'; *Her Mind's Eye* (Pyramid Press, 1996) for 'Fabulous bee'; *The Journal* for 'Anne Edgecumbe Dowriche'; *Mary Webb Society Journal* for 'Viroconium'; *Otter* for 'Somewhere'; *Ouroboros Review* online for 'Ballerina's Song of the Earth'; *Great Works Online* for 'Up on Yannadon', 'Unfinished Business' and 'Summer garden scrapblog'; *Poetry Monthly* online for 'Salix-fragilis'; *PQR* for 'Horizons', 'At Inchconnachan', 'Arachne' and 'Atropos'; *Shearsman* magazine for 'Outside there is a grene tree', 'Triune' and 'Rhys and Plath'; '1894'; *Suspension* online for 'Swell Wood'.

'Fran Skating on the Manor-Pond' was runner-up in the Exeter Poetry Prize 1999 and appeared in *Making Worlds; One Hundred Contemporary Women Poets* (Headland, 2003).

Contents

DOPPLER-EFFECTS

her eyes will green
Arachne	11
My wheel	12
Somewhere	13
Contextual	14
This is to let you know	15
Salix-fragilis	16
Swell Wood	17
Viroconium	19
Linlithgow & Mary Queen of Scots	21

blue-scape
Julia's sea-scape	23
Crag	24
Horizons	25
Pleiadian Doves	26
For those who say there are no more poems	33

TEXTUAL GROUND

Ashwood's garden	39
1849; Dean Prior	40
Summer garden scrapblog	41
Nuthatch	43
Redwing	45
Conference Table	47
1894; Fran Skating on the Manor-Pond	48
Culross visitors	49
Ballerina's *Song of the Earth*	51

shaping a phrase with a flint-tool
Devon Women	54
Cornubian Island	55
That skeletal tree	56

Take the thought	57
Musbury W/rites	58
Imagining Translation (Margaret Beaufort)	59
Anne Edgecumbe (Dowriche)	60
"Outside there is a grene tree" (Mary Lady Chudleigh)	61
Woman Clothed with the Sun (Joanna 1 and 2)	62
Up on Yannadon 1906	63
Wings (M. P. Willcocks — Novelist, 1869-1952)	64
Triune	68
Rhys and Plath: Cheriton and Court Green	71

CHANGING THE REFRACTING ANGLE

Fabulous bee	75
Chervil	77
Unfinished Business	79
Perdita	81
Atropos	82

NOTES	84

for Luke, Andrea and Jamie

Doppler-Effects

her eyes will green

Arachne

comes from a place
(beyond)   where there is
  space   here
black (drab) fields   spindle trees
   spiders in her mind
shoes clogged in earth
Her crops are few yet
she bulges   unbeaten desire for the whip
 of history retracing steps   out of mud
releasing Ariadne's thread
when she will bloom her eyes will green
   to a throbbing sky
       she will spin
            on her axis
her cobweb dress tied with a golden sash—
   over the horizon an ocean swells

My wheel
    turns

moorland vistas up by
   Hannaford

 behind its frames
   fibres
     twist

flyer of time
    rotates

 I, spinner,
left holding the yarn

(Susannah Gidley Abbott,
 Dean Prior, 1741-1823)

Somewhere

in the lining
of her head
a sepia photo, unframed,
of what her poem could be about.

In the study cobwebs
trespass over Virago books
high shelves where baby spider
plants suspend in air
her mind is sifting spaces
sewing gossamer thread
through nooks and crannies
amongst rows of women's books.

Now intent on fetching scissors
snipping ties and spinning
this imaginary yarn
of enchanted craft
she will lift her head
brush back a strand of hair
and follow spiders with that pencil,
trailing desolate landscapes
over fifty sheets of unlined paper.

Somewhere
in Devon
a run-down cottage, framed
in an old oak doorway
Father stands, his cheeks amazed
by frost,
proudly bearing in armfuls—
the last of his spring cabbage.

Contextual

I don't want annotations
for
this poem
will be
the key
simplicity

white hyacinths
sigils across grass

so
no notes
in margins—
only flowers

This is to let you know

that when I
moving with
this poetic line

saw your eyes
open upon mine
I shut the book
and ran with the page onto the open moor

Salix-fragilis

As usual
I drive through the night
my mind on you

moon is gold, full blown
hair flecks invisible
across my face.

Ghosts flicker over these marsh levels
and through the window
soundings of the armoury
of a long-ago war.

Our finale was as civil
you'd think of me
I of you.

Why should our meetings
be such as this
through liminal September evenings—

when sun and moon hover in twilight,
selves of other selves dissolve in vapours
and the lone hound
howls behind the skeletal crack-willow.

Swell Wood

Framed from the cut-out hide
little egrets gently rock their young
sky-high in heron nested ancient trees—

wind moves us
  away
from the mainstream
down the winding path
to this Other—
a dimension rustling under feet
with secret dormice in
their hidden hazel thicket

we should turn back—
the hectic road's waiting
to scoop us in its flow

but something draws us
  on
    and
further down the track—

Enchanter's Nightshade
lines the path—a galaxy of daystars
  white stones
from fairytale that led the children
to the cottage—

we must find the heart
the tick of the place
and talk of how a Circe
might lie in wait for us
 round
that next corner
where are tree-giants
ash oak and lime—

may we
be changed—
our beat chime in time with the wood.

—Watch us squirrel to the top
through the canopy out
of the scene
     to the sun.

Viroconium

> *'The past is only the present,
> become invisible'*
> (Mary Webb)

I'm sure you saw her
    —braided hair—*golden lights
rim her face* and the ring
you found at the edge of the field
after a mere hour-glass
of a mosaiced two thousand years
is spinning her longest finger.
She smiles at you as someone
(her husband) calls
across the tessellated pavement
of the palaestra:

Placida!

The name rings on
as she, slowly, turns,
her sandal-strap glistening bronze
and walks hand in hand
away with him,
across the marbled floor.
Over it a dolphin leaps,
on a fountain, into air.
They cross underworld the sea of Hades.

(Grass grows thick and crisp
through chunks of once chiselled
stone. Archaeologists come again
to explore foundations, chart on computer
the palaestra area—those colonnaded
city walls).

Fragments only left.

You noted the waft
of fragrance

as she wrapped a cloak
close round her bodice,
a jet necklace encircled her throat—
the fastening brooch is jade—

She had no voice.

At Viroconium
sheep are grazing turf
on earth covered bones—
stone haunts the museum,
inscribed:

To the gods and shades,
Placida, aged 55,
Set up by order of her husband,
In the thirtieth year of her marriage.

Space on stone
for details
of next to die.

You are born
from your more recent grave,
as you ride to her
through crested waves
on the back
of the surfacing dolphin.

Linlithgow &
Mary Queen of Scots

It's plausible then
visiting mute swans
   as ciphers might
design a uroboric circle,
     coil
lilied edges of this circumferenced lake.

Some said they'd seen ghosts
   slide swans
     in secret
round the gliding loch—
she'd return   invisible as
her writing's secret white on taffeta.

Spooked sensations then—
the cobweb bit
  was understandable
    shivery hypnotic legs adrift
     down the hollow
      of tower-rubble air.

This castle's green-grey
   moss of slime on stones
myth and story written over
and above other possible tales
of royal birthings   rapes   deaths.

She was and is the matrix,
    lode-stone
of this occulted web—

how she prays for the safety
of those who will come
   en ma fin
     est mon commencement.

Beneath darker water
   blackest
inks secrete a coagulate of thread-
worm
     eel
   water-snake.

Swans at the highest vanishing point
   way off
north of the lake
   leave a wave of wing-beat song.
We're taken aback by the ebb of this doppler effect.

blue-scape

Julia's sea-scape

I cannot trawl
your intimate seas
　your stars

　the blue healing
　of letters flax
　　flowers

rising　　like dolphins
from sea-grass

and waves
　　haul memories

the fall
　the
　　　fall

of the self

Crag

*Lichens are icicles
and blue-grey*, he says.

The hills though close
sledge minds with knife-edged paths,
streams just cool as her little running finger
over his neck and then
the tap tap tap streak
of woodpecker and scythe of kingfisher
swathing over clear water-grass.

Listen, he says again.
　Listen.
She only hears the snow
its freeze of memory blanks
and stills in the ice-box—
not the harebells whistling,
the blue-skate of mountain folds,
　cliffs slip sliding
into white-horse waters below.

Only the sea-bird calls her
cries with the shriek
of its startling lighthouse beak—

below waves beat long
　and
　　fall

Horizons

I could not speak
remembering the sky
the way now words
were shadows on the sheet
calligraphies a skein on skin
books beside held blank pages
wide-spaced horizontal lines
no more...

between us too that velvet curtain
sea
intervening always with the swelling premonition
of waves unseen
in our insanity phrases swooped
with gulls attack
we lacked the forethought then
to place between
the clean sweep of aquamarine.

and now there is a break
of sea sky and sheet
formed by blue blue blue
sky-space over a billowing midnight ocean
and sand-voiced susurration

Pleiadian Doves
Coo-coo coo-
coo-coo
coo-coo
Mornings
  high in the mirror
    in response to earth's magnetic field
from willow's golden tassels
  feather-light sleepers
    they rise
    fantasies
     high to skies
then downward
  in a silken spiral glide
   coo-coo-coo
    coo-coo

***

Usually back then
  each day
we saw just two
  though now
   flash back
we realise there were at least
    seven
     hidden
    starred
in that glassy heaven

Idly I muse—
  who are ours
which of the Pleiadian sisters
  would come down
   here
    just for us—
     Alcyone?
     Taygate?
      Celaeno?

They seemed to tease
keep a half-kept secret
coo-coo
  coo-coo-coo
    coo-coo
      we don't know really
       don't know
      though call, don't
        know

Often we'd thought their stay with us
to be lucky
 a garden-charm—
 divine messengers
they flew in to bring stalwarts
 peace
   hope
joy

though sometimes
 in silhouette their preying shape
made them instead
   sinister
sparrow-hawks
 a threat

One night in a dream
   the dyad appeared
  revealed the significance
  of their cooing cryptograph
    they spoke as one
of their dovian constellation—

Our elliptical elegance
  reflects
our ancient choric origins
the repeat refrain's
 a collective muse
on the fixity of our fate—

*the conflation of our life's journey
with that of women's archaic past*

*Not your usual couple
  of Darby
    & Joan
  two lost sister souls
we've become ciphers
for remembering those who
tend always to be forgot*

*Agreed you might have heard of Electra
but Celaeno what d'you know of her?
—our dark one
she mothered a king who founded city states
or Alcyone—she of the mystic light
who Poseidon stole
or even solitary Taygate
founder of Sparta
some say she took her own life
after Zeus pursued her*

*Our daily visits to your garden
are as sojourners only
we may not be what you think we are
  and indeed
even we double our quest
  each day
    and night
as soon as light's last click
  has left this space
we lift from our straggly platform-
nest
      rise
  high
    glide   to sky
in a fleeting blink of dove-eye
as evening segues to darkest night
we meet up with our Pleiadian sisters
and soar in an arc*

*Our flight takes us
over the curve of Perseus
to Orion's Belt
there's Aldebaran
  in the east
then we are home
every star-constellated night
we extend our Pleiadian wing's
  white sail
  out across the Milky Way
resume the pattern of our fixed sigil
our iconographic display
to remind earth's inhabitants
of what and who we are
    and why we stay*

*We float our delicate dipper-net
  stars
        pivot
of the universe
though often now in so-called
modern times
we're not seen*

  *Lost
in the haze of city-lights
where there should be sky-
hieroglyph space
  is black abyss—
the faintest smudge
on a woman's granddaughter's
treasure-chart of night
  we dissolve
  into the impregnations
of your artificial
    skies*

*No one notices
when earth's covered
with a shroud of cloud*

for a dove moment
  we waft
 across the nebulae
   and visit Cassiopeia

We let her go
she's free to roam for an hour
you might just spot us
when you think you see
that white angel
  satellite
 lit from behind

We intend one night
to whirl the chair aright
help Cassiopeia end her
sentence—
she can return to earth
where she belongs
 boast her vanity
  show off her finery

She is the oracle

Then as time curves back
to heliacal return of day
and sun's anacrychal rise
we spiral-shape our path along
air-current's visual grids

reconfigure our bird-selves
 on that golden willow perch
 preen in the reflecting mirrors
  of your room

It's not that we intend
 to deceive
 and you must believe
  we pass our day
  without a care

*we're contemplating yogis
 on the high-rise wire*

*Truth is we're waiting
  watching
   hoping
to meet up with our long-lost
abandoned friend
    Artemis*

*You might have noticed
our extended family
  our avatars
   our replicas
    our mates   our flock
have spread across
the local map   its garden
colonised its garden space—
though one of us was irretrievably lost
 some time ago
  when she fell
    to someone else's garden
      perished
  amongst the petals of its whitest rose*

*Our sigil is now a little dimmer
  even than before—*

*We hope to find Artemis
our beloved and elusive sister
  in a secret sunlit grove
there we will compare
  and reconcile
    our layered pasts*

***

*Coo-coo-coo
coo-coo*

Some nights
a certain slant—

moon-
glyph light-

  shadows
hover
  up
  across
 the outside traceries
of willow-twigs
   rise
  high
    higher
 into skies
out of sight
  out of mind
coo–coo
  coo–coo–coo

For those who say there are no more poems

1
Look at these swallows
an intoxication of loops—
and under
 blue

  headlong

   dives
over butterfly-skims above
the whites of this green gold field

It's easy to miss them—
they sail close to the wind—
to misunderstand the
turn of their phrase,
the twisted spell of their
secret code

and what can you say
of the white under-belly flash
silking those exquisite plaits of wheat?

2
Tell them how it was
for us not so long ago
in a world where

there were no…
mobile phones [*phone-home home-phone
Phone Home*]

MP3s MP4s
Nintendos
YouTubes iTunes
Facebooks smartphones

No Phone-home home-phone
  Home...

where home was a place
not a meeting-site in virtual space...

  Phone...

3
It's calm tonight
we're floating on a sea a wheat-green
gold alchemy
each stalk waving a soul from
underworlds where fallow deer
swim a fox prowls
and you imagine you can see
the baiji dolphin— even re-imagine
  Persephone—

You wonder what
she is doing
the schedule she set with
her mother and Hadeian
Underground lover
has, after all been going on
for quite a while

(and earth is still going round)

No she's probably having
a hedonistic time—out of it
on ecstasy—and forgotten long ago
what she came back for
or got bored enticing
those poor souls beneath

She's obviously content
with her lot—lover keeps her happy,
doesn't need her dose of sun
and sky—

*or, she's fed up being
a tool between Mother
and lover not wanting anymore
to do their dirty work*

*She'll drowse in the home
of her deep earth-bed
heady with day-dream
sleep and idylls of night
on bedded rock for another 2000 years—
so many poems will enter her head
only fragments
seep up to ground as
white-wheat seeds—
they'll pick them up with flints*

*until mother and lover
resolve their differences*

4
Today I watched the swallows
violet-black their midday
swoop
over shadow and field

and a white belly uplift
to the perch on phone-lines and on to Shangri-la
through broken skies—(they're after all
above it all a hieroglyphic sign from God)

5
…where Home was not
a place in space

and poet was
a Poet

Textual Ground

Ashwood's garden

...
  and besides not known as gardener
    the writer
looks for hidden words in plants
    and flowers

her summer-house sanctuary's
  an ode of ivy   margins
embroiled with ragwort
    and wild-oat strewn corn

Someone has to come
  risk the electric-fence
spray the superfluity of weeds
and chasten the poisoned chalice
    of this place

where at the heart
  lies an art
    that cajoles
this sharpened pencil to chisel chosen paths

1849; Dean Prior

Every evening
    sundown
he stands at the vegetable plot's
       foot
shadowed by wood's dark gorge

 Abbot's Way's weaving its ancient path
 across
    Lamb's Down

out along his own past grandfathers stretch   behind him

(John Abbott, Woolcomber, 1769-1853)

Summer Garden Scrapblog

This Garden
could be virtual
evidence of a Second-Life—
a web designed for another
self who wants to walk
a shadow along its twisted paths,
then meet her once true-self
returning to her own back door

> *hostas in clay-pots   scrolled blue sea-blue lavender slug devoured flowers Holy the host … ess is behind closed doors Hosta Host this ghost hostile sometime   she will try hospitality…*

Blackbird
could thrill her
to an everywhere-garden, its
dapple across a childhood-green
no need of patterned order then—
*you didn't notice bindweed how it clung death over and around
that Danse du Feu*, the avatar says

> *…and are the roses   sick how worms   turn   squirming along earth tunnels worm-holed   we   seek another universe   where we can sing in the trellis   with the wrens…*

Columbine
how split her purple thoughts—
aquilegias a crack of seeds
from bonnets where she walks in lavender-fields
and breaking words arrive in single letters
on a blank page

> *…you try and spell them   in this blue reflecting sky   there even the
> sentence   is a mirage
> mirrored by that ramshackle wire-grass yard-grass goose-grass
> disturbance in the field…*

Summerhouse
wild by this tree
there's a house of stories
patterned in dappled shade
under the oak—the Jet splits ears
and tells another tale

> *...Aah a woman's screaming ecstasy   skateboards the street
> agony not knowing from where she flew
> who would hear her cries or who would note them in a moving blog...*

Gunnera
Monster you're a jungle animal
giant with green-splayed hands
how you crush our fan-tail fish
these images drown as soon as thought
yet how I long to be
a sprite cradled in the lap
of your palm

> *...stepping back by verbena   seeds sewn as words in ground   the garden
> room   red geraniums neatly lined in pots on sill one or two leaves heart-
> shape the mind she will will it on to flower...*

Nuthatch

We remember to feed them
crumbs of comfort
during fresh falls of snow

take time to become attuned
note this snowfield
is not just ours

She hops the fence from the copse below
 her usual high-wire balancing act
is on the snow-lichened oak—

though reclusive she's not
silent.
 Diva

of the garden
she announces her arrival
chit-chit

trills over and over
her signature call
chit-chit chit-chit

adds an extended melisma
chit-acc cacciaccatura
 acciac-
  catura—

the grace of
her flawless song
hovers still in air

flutter-tonguing white
 with the wafers
communing us

—this garden
　with the manna
　of her haven

Redwing

will she hop over
    again
as that winter we had a visitor
  just once
    in the garden

over the hedge her siblings
  feasted
    on skimmias

 shy she didn't stay long
it was the coldest January that decade
   snows had just arrived

crimson berries plump
 with sweet juice
strung their necklace across grass' white page

   *

 bird dips
on the twig of branch
twists to us a red
glyph
   wing
zee-it zee-up zee-it!

she could be delivering a secret
cryptic warning
  a gift
another white feather
 for us to keep
inside our special closed-book

when we're ready
  one day
we'll use it to complete our half-
 written Book of Life

*

this time she doesn't want
   to join us
her flock calls
in the depths of night

as they pass again
   on the wing
     loop to follow
the power of turning trade-winds

far away from here
back to the icelands

zee-up zee-
 it! zee-it!

Conference Table

Against the white-scape
 this twig
  network

winter stems
 flame
  their tangle
midwinter's fire

Performing sparrows
rattle around branch
 labryinths

deftly working
 their *Cornus* room
  they

        rip
        &
        dart

   seeds   nut-
  food for thought

whilst
 alone
  solitary
  survivor
  robin
  stakes
   red
  his claim
       warns
     half-
       flies half
     hops
the wide divide
  between
sustaining twig
 and table

1894: Fran Skating on the Manor Pond

She skates over and around its frozen surface,
then spins a pencil-pirouette,
muffs blue-heat her hands
and from her waist a scarlet whirl of skirt.
In hazy light veins seem to break in olive eyes
as the blades of her boots refract the scratching ice
and under setting sun
her shadow is half a pulsating heart.

Ida, in the kitchen sits and snips
the corners of the paper folds.
Brittle like ice.
Deft, her fingers snip and snap then
rippling like a fan the row of skating dolls
holding hand by hand.

Robert, in the other room
turns a page.
His book about the Ministry
is a weight upon his mind.

His sisters are making their mark;
each enacts a secret lore
on a slated sheet of white,
figure skating on the land of open-space
and inscribing a serrated pictograph.

Even the tiny feet of each minute dancing doll
are chipped away to equip them with the sharpest razor cut.

Culross visitors

smoke
  a low shroud
was once keening
  north from the Forth

now on a clear day
from hanging gardens—
  where lavender, alchemilla and old
roses ramble   sweet-scented
  roots
held firm in ancient earth

and sun light   over red-pantiled roofs   ochre walls—

behind Grangemouth
you can see clouds
soft purple-
veiled hills
Pentlands fadeback east
into Lammermuirs

  you might
think of those once nubile girls
  how their needles swift flit in
    out   cloth covered in
garden colour crewel-worked
  with chains
      daisies
    secret-motifs

  and if you read the pages
at the back of the books
you might even
  just
consider
other earlier visitors

one turret right at the top of that house

there in the garret
shut away from sun
and light day-on-
day and
 night-
on-night
   kept
from sleep

women   known as
  witches
scratching
   signs
     daisies
        stars
 sigils of betrayed beliefs

day-by-day dreaming
of that one night sail
  in cockle shells
on the calm wake of a forever
    grey-
blue Lammermuir mirror.

Ballerina's 'Song of the Earth'
(for Darcey Bussell)

Someone draws
a circle
pencil-line ornate in grey

around that empty space
the virtual (veritable) land

where no one is
except
a bird (lost bride)

 butterfly
free from its cage

      *

Have you ever (just once)
considered latent (wasted) talent
where words are lost-in-ether
though they may alight on a limb
of branch or perch as sigil on the stalk
of a rose?

Where does the phrase of incomplete text
finish? How long
does it exist in air before
it dies or
drops
to earth dead
stone?

      *

And no! She couldn't have been there!
All a figment and that   you know don't you
what I mean?   though
bracken was an arena for theatre

The day I saw her on the moor
I'd been considering the
Self
fulfilment
those who say
they can have
and do
everything anything
as and when
they like   and thinking
how fortunate they must be

Just to the north   high on the crown
of Sorton tor there's a metamorphosis
of rocks   beneath my feet
this moor-scape edge   grass-hillocks on
green-earth salted with dew

   *

She sashayed
down from mid-grey skies—Ballerina!

You must have seen her
dancing
on the ground—

demi-plié—
pirouettes on pointe

catch light on her dress
as she skims
  & spirals
her dervish of whirling death

it's chiffon and satin a border
of organdie and net
 shimmer
of lilac-cerise

blue

  sequins

    butterflying

      everywhere

She's intent on inner voices
singing the song
where she went on the night of her final
Farewell to Earth

I caught the last glimpse
her terre à terre   before
she'd gone   one with the hang-glider
behind the tor
the stones
out of view
of sight

and now don't know
if she came to be part of the poem
to tell us something
or even flew in just for fun
a trick of light   simplicity itself
disguised in a moving text
of ballet-dress

You do know—
She won't return.

shaping a phrase with a flint-tool

*Devon
Women; Lost W/rites;
Sonnets
& Impressions*

Web designed for another self
who wants to walk back with others' shadow

and walking through the front oak-door back into a room and table
by a morning lit window at which (she) who is me wrote

*here a stem snowdrop   in clear glass
a flint shining in red earth*

Cornubian Island

White clouds are allowed
as are the shredded grey of gulls
and bracken fronding edge of fields

a voice is thin trailed sea-weed

these shapes script on sand
a biblical text
  women's narratives
score the landscape; torn; dissected
  lost
an amethyst stone is key
its blue rites are gems red
 over
empty pages tumbling under coastal waters.

That skeletal tree

 is a signature
writing its reams across a landscape hole
grey-slate language sharpens the peninsula
words implode that night parole
under a zig-zag crossing zone of sky

   Columba Cassiopeia Andromeda
each watches over—an angelic gaze—
a woman star (above and so below)

This patch of earth is mirrored by that dome
a trajectory shadowed curvature of place
beneath   hidden at rest in unvisited graves
fragments of bones   of words
   hardly a trace

Take the thought

                of correspondence
of colour coded strata rock arching
above a salted, singing Thetis sea.
An agate swirl; tip of a tern wing
over aquamarine waves; that hush and ssh
of tide's convolution; its renewing
trawl of patterned texts; its nets'
recall of multilingual fish. Fling
shoals—caught words—into the deep
secreted ocean bed; a cauldron turns
and turns about the creature of the coming neap
tide's fathoming depths; the runes it leaves
are tarnished silver, but glitter gold around
the margins. What is left only found.

Musbury W/rites

The pen maps a path
up and over these sheep-grazed tracks
below a church tower
under mist is Atlantis or Aberdovey
above a bank skirts
crumbling ridges some gorse
a clump of pine trees   Black ink
sketches lines of thought   a skeletal
maze across this Devon hill where
rabbit holes dissect scorched grass
and where up there a figure
silhouetting the cusp of hill shadows
those who have stood beside their muse
before   Wondering   at ritual
Parallel these lines shot
across fields reflected in night skies
or muffled under earth   only
ground tremors shift time
back to then   Now
and a woman clothed in cloth
the colour of berries
shaping her phrase
with a flint-tool
on the resin-scented conifer
turns
from her poem and
carves her way
back the tracks
up to the inner circle

Imagining Translation; Margaret Beaufort

(Click, double click click, click click click.) Moving
through space virtually frame by frame, tubular
tunnels, phrase by phrase, through textual palimpsests
year by year to the void of the past, where spatially
her story perhaps began. Even the Book
was then as good as new. She lived and worked
with Latin texts; once dissected, selected the equivalent
felicitous phrase. Manuscripts
  meticulously set
by the first print press were stored in vaults at old
archival sites. They're ISP lit up from that
original source. Now, imagining translation
her textual lines are sifting in, snatched
from gaps in this shifting chimera,
its parchment pages, rich medieval illumination
words written between the covers of her book
  of blacke velome

She knew the sign of her corrupted nature the battle that will crown her son is to the east and only years away she is Grandmother of later queens swete herbs strew her chambers   thus she is here in a state of grace, cognisant of the mirroure of her infinite reflection becoming a chiasmatic tree   shredded into history in 1509 she travelled along the tracks of Old Devon   swete herbs strewe her chambers   her treasures in the county are many her estates on this peninsula space as rich as royalty   her stays in the county were perhaps brief yet her influence spreads far and wise   not her own words   no voice of her own solely translation   linguistic insights chasing future generations…

Anne Edgecumbe (Dowriche)

I can find you only through your fathers, husband,
nephew, brother, sons; you could seek yourself
through only male personae, his prose texts;
your mother won't stop swopping names;
your niece is you (you might be in her grave).
There's a portrait on the upper corridor
of the house your father built. Girl.
Unknown. (Of the family; of the time).
I would that she was you. Her kirtle
is folded pleat over pleat upon pleat,
the overskirt's taffeta sheen a surprise sage-green
and that stolid stare from where you
    follow your future
round and around the upper landing, letting
the steps of visitors repeat themselves
into emptiness, whilst the inked
hollows of your eyes remain, black and still…

Tapestries told from tales these names appear and vanish thin thin thin air when doves spin and sky thick with chocked words still blue names come and go hidden in elaborately branched trees where fine veiled leaves drop to cold grounds hidden as our/are cuboid boxes secret in these cossetted escritoires your little fingers tempted by tiny clasps tantalise and open find behind another hidden compartment your writing habits here ingrained in ebony boxes of history and the house turns in on itself looks inwards the temenos its inner enigmatic space where history can not find that inner courtyard where you grew a tudor flower you will always be peeping from your father's Solar through the recessed secret window on the perimeters the outer guard rooms closely protect your family mysteries armour plated arrows rapiers men in your life threatened with them yet you knew where to sidle away to find the hidden passageways tunnels under-ground little spaces like places where poems spelt themselves into invisible sigils in your head the tapestry will continue to tell your stories

"Outside there is a grene tree": Mary Chudleigh; Ashton

no Saint present in the porch. a gap
in the trefoil-headed niche, "et exultavit infans
in utero eius" *I see but cannot ease her pain*

today the nave's shadow shapes a cradle,
we are swept through dust to dust of ions
family secrets are hidden on ledger stones

saints on the rood-screen Sidwell's scythe
blood still spurts *I still her dying conflict view
the sad sight does all my grief renew*

in the east wall cavity the rosette
and fragment of carved stone a flake
of angel's wing   the inner sanctuary

*She meekly lies, gazes on me with eyes
that beg belief but all in vain,
I see, but cannot, cannot ease her pain.*

Woman clothed with the Sun: Joanna

As then, two hundred years before,
thoughts turn to Apocalypse.
Inclement weather now,
the world in terror then. Pandora's
red delights are thrilling earth… A
quiet voice caresses
still those sunlit scenes, translating
Eden's garden
onto richest Devon's fields. God had
chosen to announce the Second
Coming and the snake's ubiquitous in
long grass.

> *Despise not prophecies or those who can*
> *foretell the shooting star… Now I'll tell*
> *them what to do. Just prove the writings, they*
> *are true. Unfasten cords from the Box*
> *within that Great Box of Common Wood;*
> *in the inner Arc white-bound with ribbon find*
> *sealed rich bundles of texts. Read Sigils for*
> *healing earth from these leaves of the Tree of Life.*

Look for the Key. At the apposite
moment
all'l be revealed—a dream-bird's flight
across Midnight Skies or a
conflagration. Sudden. Startling. Of
the ancient oak tradition.

Joanna (2)

Some said she was charismatic,
enigmatic; others, eccentric, fanatic,
an impostor. Choose for yourself.
Hear the story, seal the fate
of the Woman of the Revelation. Her
son, Divine Child, was to be born and
succoured on the State-Bed; its frame
satinwood, embroidered with gold.

> *The canopy's ornamented with*
> *morning and evening stars, a*
> *gold dove at its centre preens*
> *the olive branch of peace; blue*
> *silk stitched with blue thread is*
> *shimmering over the cradle-*
> *crown: intricate carving and a*
> *gilt sheen beneath.*

The layette, daytime frocks, night
flannels: linen; muslin caps and
flannels for a coat; those tiny silver
brocaded shoes.

So Shiloh, Prince of Peace. Devil
of the piece was located in a
disease of the uterus: size of a small
pear, thus dissected relic of her
mission.

Up on Yannadon; June 1906

Who was Edith   leaving *The Grange*
    went for a walk
        a long walk   up and in-   *red-admiral*
to   the dip above
that clear golden sky   rare   orchids   *painted-*
in her hand   those   flowers   *lady*
    in her hair   and how oh
how   they issue
    a sneeze
        of coloured tissue   flit   *wall-butterfly*
with us   ghost-moths
far away from the falsity of   *peacock-*
collections   from our own   *butterfly*
 scarlet   cosmetic-box
    to a place
        Nirvana
          where E.M.H.
  who was Edith
     who left for a stroll   round the fields   went
for many   a long walk   many
another long   long   walk   with fragrant   *orange-*
golden blossom   under sky   *tipped*
her carpet   blinging   blue-
bells   primrose   spurge   and up on the moor
  she followed paths with   her soft
butterfly   brushes   taking   her pencil for a longer walk
  to   sketch and write texts that
     narrate her birds   beasts   flowers
her world of sky and gorse   soaring lark   and
  the hawk sailing into
                the sea of gold   above
 setting sun   following

this everlasting long walk   a future towards
the death-branch   above grey water   hovering
    waving
      hook   back   ensnare her

    tortoise-shell   *spotted-orchid*   *wild-*
                                              rose

Wings
M. P. Willcocks
1869-1952

*Life is an ocean on which we are all carried,
star systems, birds, beasts, and men the living and
those who are to them but names on a tombstone (MPW)*

I have to take another's alien world and gaze out where is the dead author her libido is cosmic countless constellations finely-tuned extra-spatial in dimension intricate her biosphere her writing must keep going as she in all directions multi-versed dispersals into other words a new child recent poem fresh text different universe. Explodes (everything is in the word) creating texts resuscitated in a novel guise dark water matters in a many folded universe altering her imaginary order she's interacting with particles waves from other sites in space-time a system of signs wax works of subjects in process these fictional avatars figures in a dream tiny iridescent bubbles in time's space they stutter twirl waft—away dandelions futuristic seeding skies... [floating text]

...Heart-beat: a clock and all else silent in this room
she's trying to find felicitous words
to delineate a writer who's there beside her
and begins to write herself back
into the place where she was born
there was once a child
who set out to find *the land of blue distance*
...*strange blue hills remained*
...as far away...
beyond the folded blue
on pleated purple folds of moor...

Incantations: Joanna MacGregor recital 2002

```
Pandora opening a grand-piano's wing
      hollow
            oscillations of this reverberation
                        over-toned
                              shaped bars
                              beat far flung     corners
                              (black widow spiders  lurk)
drifts and fills a concert hall     in waves
      evaporates       warps-in-space
      pulsates          an/y Other universe
                              sonata's sounding
            absent           phonics dissolving blue
                        ritardando blue to
                              shadow blue  incantations
                              lured by a cadential figure
                                    caught
in a framework of suspended time      a sympathy
      of resonance
                        we    move beyond ourselves into sonic selves
                              other selves sequestered in this manifestation
                                    of the moment of all time
```

Wings

1902: novel; London; concert. A pianist
Sarah Bellow interprets *Appassionata Inspiritrice*
this recital's reinstating her career—*the old
went back to memories, young forward
to their future, for her playing dealt with the song
the voice sings to the soul*—she'd been away
at the site of her writer's dream—for four years lost
In that magic-space of hypertext, hyper-linked long note
of silence absent in a sound within another world
in multiverse transported—mercury shifted
through a futured time-warp. 2002: sister,
a pianist, wraps Sarah beneath her angel-wing.
In the web-cam they exchange sound-tips,
extemporize manuscript inscriptions on runic stones;
in this 3D soundscape their solid ground
is the violaceous throw cast over this late summer moor.

Will o' the wisp… I try to find
you on that ancient moorland track
that rambles to a figment of a virtual world
knowing you were—and are—as she
who charmed and created you,
now in disrepute. It could be as simple
as finding a feather or agate moss
on a stone at the base of this rock:
look, a universe unravels from the protonema's
green threads; or gazing up through blue-air
that lark's angled wing-tip is a new sun
shimmering auras of heat-haze; even
this rock crystal rose quartz
enfolds air bubbles wherein you are hidden:
like the Queen of Sheba, *not a woman,
but a world*, spinning within… the *will o' the wisp*

Triune

You can see them shaped in the frame looking through the window they are on the threshold at the projection of this Devonian land: she stares eastward over into her own future; her concerns only in the west with those that have passed; between the both catching the thread, she's for ever sitting in the window, completing her book, without end...

Freya

is Artemis attuned to earth
new land   cone-shaped   a volcano
opens every morning over the eastern brow

of Meldon Hill   nose to peat ground
she's discovering buried cities in the husks of silt
and sand   yet curiously oblivious to lost voices

of invisible fates she's immersed in this landscape
the source of the starting points of life's journey
a future for travel yet grounded in moor

and steeped with its bones   Stones
in her pocket weigh forever her way
salt to dust-earth   Moor is her playground   Prelude

Treasure   later she will make her own map
text uncoiling in a long ravishing italic sigil
over shadier foreign lands   *At last Arabia!*

Frances

How aware she is of hushed voices
warning of those future years of wracking pain
Her house desolate   unsettled as the now rare texts

but in her mind a bijouterie of words
She knows of those in mist   they sift
with early ghostly shifts on water

notes voices listening on stone and
light's gaze through grass from the brink
of moor   thus found she can't write

her soul's on a trip somewhere
else   assailed by death and its intricate choice
of paths   Herself one of the undead dead

she's saved by those she's always
comforted   wild animals of earth
tortoise   cat   owl   moth

lampyridae blaze their singing trails
Her poems are encrypted
where her mind's a lark
over Roborough Down

She's watching sunsets
quivering on the shafts of light

Lux eterna   Lux eterna

Beatrice

at her window describes the rainbow high behind Hound-Tor back
Afternoon   she climbs Bonehill Down   her high-laced boots
 Spring
    on peat   beneath
  Shadows   limestone caves   an age when mammoths roamed

She is and will be remembered   Matriarch of the Moor
now her girth surmounts an east to west moorland circumference
heavy that gait   solid the texturing green tweed overskirt

sweeping boulders and brooks   watch her squat
 over bracken   *purple moor*   the *sweet vernal grass*
   crossleaved heath   a-swirl of sigils on rock
her belly a crevice
    the issuing wound of words

Slow   Eternal
this rich fermentation
         the textual ground.

Rhys and Plath: Cheriton and Court Green

these two at least are drawn toward the heart
not by pulsating blood   were always set apart
agendas written   memories of other coasts
sand-salted air   sea-spray shiftings   ghosts
pursued animal tracks   footsteps they knew
allowed bone instinct   renewed
a tug of roots towards our far west coast
each found a home   a haven   her most
aerial   though anchored   texts spilled out
over night-time tables   dispelling doubt
and fear   these hit hardest during days
when sheep grazed fields in Devon space displaced
the given self its fretted folds and pleats
to fractured arteries   that beat beat beat.

Changing
the refracting angle

Fabulous bee

A fabulous bee... sprung into vision
blotting out the edge of the stables
almost blotting out the sun itself (Her, H.D.*)*

Of course
it is all a matter of perspective
just getting things the right size
and not seeing what's not there.

It seemed
 a good system,
revolving double stars
and eyes keeping track
of other eyes close in orbit—
from either side of the axis
equal shadowed angles
slanting the sun-dial
the meridian crossed.

We knew identical time
and space
          only gradually did I
moving away
put words into the gap
and see the empty dream of seas
as veils drew back
and sunsets dropped illusions
into hallucinated light
looked through the telescope
the wrong way
saw your eyes
 mysteriously
dilate
a star apparently
 contract.

As I said
it is about proportion, representation,

all I see of what I now observe
is the flow of a reel of colour-printed memories
one enlarged—
always that white heat light behind
you striding fiercely up the path
holding out an amber rose
and sometimes, now, another figure
bends, stoops slightly over,
crosses the angle

of straining light
 tiger is slaying tiger
in forest recesses of that night.

Chervil

*Plant this picture
in a whorl of mind,
start to invite,
to re-invoke
that buried
beneath scattered
interpretative stones.
Recall wiser meanings.*

Sun is full—
ripening through chervil half-light,
an effect chequering flowerings
of *Queen Anne's lace* and *Torilis japonica*.
In the shade of this new century hedge
cars spin by, stir dust, expel fumes.
Air's exhausted.

Whirling, the mind
turns and scatters stones,
oblivious to tiny hiding insects
and brushes of grass caressing skin.

Shut out, its undertow of past-life memories;
they flit across the brain,
hair strands flickering a white page
when, bent over the table, in sun,
thought lights catch the unfolding poem
changing the refracting angle…

**a woman ago times   a witch   at dawn   in mist
picks and swallowes the sharpe blacke seed   sees
herself reflect another half-lit self   in a shadowed
chervil hedge   this vision double spins   her
long hands curl the wand   and the mirror turns
with the waxing moon**

*Recall wiser meanings;
how the wise woman*

achieved her vision.
Flecked were her eyes
reflecting the self of the double life
and from her lips,
charm of the words of the temulentum

Unfinished Business
for Chrissy Banks & i.m. Tony Charles

As I remember
  and your dual texts always
  and ever will
confirm

there we were
sitting   writing in black
somehow   poetic osmosis I guess
we'd all agreed
beforehand
to dress as for a funeral w/rite

  but then in a group of friends
  someone has to go
first

amongst prosaic notes I jotted
the rimming of reflection
your and your
shadowed eyes
scratched out from
these   *garish hideous*

exotic flowers
left in
waiting to be
stitched
or embroidered tightly
into a final wreath

Now   nearly twenty years
later   looking for
something else   other
past drafts
  finding these
lines

how they pop-up
from the abandoned book
I understand why I was reluctant to share
I look at words you can not see

It is as then

I didn't couldn't know
the reason for this rite

   though as I said
   someone had to go
   first others
   left to bear the fruit

couldn't know

we share a barrel of biscuits bottle of wine
still together the three of us
music breathing the clock

I closed the book
blacked its message

until now

when this poem heaves itself
from the sheaf of neglected notes
replete with a foretaste of grief
yet   new *the baby thrusts out its fist*

Perdita

<pre>
has lost her way into the future   in the green westcountry woods
         she sinks   into oaks   this is the ice age
         drift   leaves are frozen
     white   crisp   edges sting her skin   she has no blanket
there are no paths in this wood
     to direct her way   few birds
                                              doves
     high up
        in fir trees   icicles glisten
             beaks are frozen
                        she kneels   peers
over a precipice   has narrowly missed a bad fall
  into the past   misadventure follows her
               a wasp buzzing
         behind her thin shoulders
                    she sees what she thought was lost for ever
             Perdita's father is
                     memory   she sees rubbles stones in loose pile
stacked from past to future   stone mountains some about to topple
                  land subsides
   stone beneath seas and under earth dug up by invisible forces
            and she saw
stones inscribed with texts that ran with the inks of intricate veining
       the ancient
                  most hallowed trees in the wood
         you might see and read them here on the surface
           may hear the music loop
              counterpoint   behind the surreptitious text
</pre>

Atropos

path forwards   locked   this train of words
which has to end   a chain of keys   her prison cell
(ways and phrases blocked)   she skirts around
the crumbling walls   issues on her mind perspectives
close   and intersect   confined   to a narrowed
point   her life is but a paint of shreds   shimmer
of fly-blue   dust of cobwebs and the webbed thread
dancing   behind the pupa of her eyes   in and out
betwixt between   that skein of unkempt words
      she holds
scissors   soon   soon she will   Snip

The little skipping girl is reflecting on the white
magnolia ceiling. She knows answers. She can wait.

Notes

p.49 CULROSS VISTORS
In the C17, suspected witches were imprisoned in the attic of the Town House at Culross.

p.51 BALLERINA'S *SONG OF THE EARTH*
Bussell's last performance with the Royal Ballet in June 2007 was Kenneth MacMillan's ballet *Song of the Earth*.

p.54 SHAPING A PHRASE WITH A FLINT TOOL
This sequence, a work in progress, centres on the subject of women writers with links to Devon and the South West. To begin with, my intention was to write each poem loosely constructed as a sonnet for every one of the selected writers. However, gradually snippets of language took off in various directions; the poems refused to conform. Different voices surfaced, disappeared and re-emerged; some were fragmentary, others lyrical, some arrived as visual images. The multilayered text mirrors the historical canonic status of women writers from the south-western region. Frequently forgotten, details of many lives and texts are hidden in archival depths away from the public eye; when they do surface, they are fragmentary, inchoate and interwoven with other lives and texts.

p.55 CORNUBIAN
A term from geological literature, used since 19th century. The Cornubian island was a palaeogeographical feature of South-West England during the Jurassic and Cretaceous periods. See *Transactions of the Devonshire Association*, vol. 131.

p.59 IMAGINING TRANSLATION — MARGARET BEAUFORT
Lady Margaret Beaufort, Countess of Richmond, 1450-1509, Henry VII's mother, inherited several Devon manors; she is said to have stayed in the house that still overlooks the church.

p.59 ...*the Book was then as good as new*

Printing was still a new art; William Caxton set up his printing press under her protection and printed books at her request and expense. One of the earliest of these was *Blanchardine and Eglantine*.

p.59 ...*She lived and worked with Latin texts*
Margaret Beaufort loved literature; she translated several texts. These included *The Mirroure of Gold*.

p.60 ANNE EDGECUMBE / DOWRICHE
Anne Edgecumbe/Dowriche was the C16 Devonian writer of the long narrative poem *The French Historie*. She probably spent her childhood

at Mount Edgcumbe—as it is now spelled—which her father Richard Edgecumbe (1528-1622), built in the mid C16. Line 2: her husband was Hugh Dowriche, vicar of Honiton from 1587-98; her brother was Piers Edgecumbe, the then Sheriff of Devon; her eldest son, William, is mentioned in her father in law's will: he is bequeathed "a silver goblet and £5". Anne is mentioned in this will as "The wife of my saide son Hugh". He leaves to "my well beloved daughter in law Ann Dowriche—fore pounds of lawful money of England to make her a rynge". Line 3: *The French Historie* is narrated through the persona of an Englishman who encounters a French protestant exile while strolling in the woods. Dowriche informs her readers that her sources for the poem are obtained from texts written by men: these are in the main based on Machiavellian ideas recently introduced to England by such writers as Innocent Gentillet. Line 4: Anne's mother was thought to be Margaret Luttrell, from Dunster, who was actually Anne's sister in law. Now it is assumed that Anne's mother was Elizabeth, from the Tregian family of Golden Manor in Cornwall. Line 5: The sources have also confused Anne Dowriche and her niece Anne, daughter of Piers, who married Richard Trefusis. Line 6: The portrait at the time of writing was on the top landing at Mount Edgcumbe: the identity of the sitter is unknown. A tapestry at Cotehele is said to represent the marriage of Richard Edgecumbe to Elizabeth Tregian.

p.61 'Outside there is a grene tree' — Mary Chudleigh
The C17 poet Mary Lady Chudleigh lived near and worshipped at Ashton church. Quotations are from her poem, 'On the Death of my Dear Daughter Eliza Maria Chudleigh'. St Sidwell is represented on Ashton Church's C15 screen.

p.62 Woman Clothed with the Sun — Joanna Southcott
Joanna Southcott (b. Gittisham, Devon 1750, d. 1814), was the Westcountry prophet, visionary and so-called greatest religious phenomenon of her age. At her death she left an infamous *Box of Sealed Writings*. Joanna believed she was the woman clothed with the sun of the Book of Revelation. When she was 64 she declared that she was pregnant with the Messiah by means of immaculate conception: she died four months later; dissection after death revealed no pregnancy, but instead flatulence and "extensive omental fat". Words in italics are adapted from Southcott's own writings and descriptions of Southcottian ephemera taken from a display at Exeter's Royal Albert Memorial Museum. The illustration is from a photo taken inside Gittisham church.

p.64 Up on Yannadon
Edith Holden, author of *The Country Diary of an Edwardian Lady* and *Nature Notes* stayed at The Grange, Dousland, on Dartmoor and walked

daily on the moors. She drowned in a backwater of the Thames at the age of 29, having fallen in whilst trying to reach a branch laden with chestnut buds.

p.65 WINGS

M.P. Willcocks, born in Devon, was a prolific writer. In several novels Willcocks spoke of "hauntings" and this sequence is intended to suggest synchronicity between two parallel space-times; a text now can relate to a text then: Perhaps, amongst multiple universes, in synchronicity, phenomena can be linked by the silence of two sounds from two different worlds in space-time. Sarah (pianist-heroine from Willcocks' 1912 novel *Wings of Desire*) is in her "dream next-door": in a parallel universe, she can return to the moor; or she can come to the present, her future, and to pianist Joanna MacGregor's concert. Though a character created by Willcocks, she is still present, even if her author has been forgotten; if we posit multiverses, then those imaginary fictional worlds and characters may each be from another (real) world—as figures in a dream or a little bubble in space-time. Ideas and sounds from beneath—words ghosted behind words—infiltrate the upper poem as thought-links between the two pianists and personalities, Joanna (real world) and Sarah (fictional). At the beginning, the poet tries to find the forgotten writer. The final is Dartmoor, at the heart of the landscape of Willcocks' writing (she "is" the moor). The phrase "there was once a child" and other words in italics in 'Wings' are taken from Willcocks' own texts.

p.68 FREYA

Freya Stark (1893-1993), travel writer, essayist, photographer, Arabist, adventurer, autobiographer. In *Traveller's Prelude*, she wrote of sitting in the bay of her bedroom at her father's house on Dartmoor, looking through the window and imagining her future travels. *At Last Arabia* is the title of one of Stark's ravishing accounts of her travels to the then most exotic places on earth; she is drawn to the Orient and her twenty travel books include maps of uncharted regions of Arabia.

p.69 FRANCES

Frances Bellerby, 1899-1975, poet and fiction writer, lived at Clearbrook on Dartmoor from 1951-1955. Early in marriage, a cliff fall left her with a permanent back injury and in 1950, Frances was diagnosed with breast cancer. In her poem 'It is not likely now', she looks west from the bedroom window of her cottage: "a great fleet jewels the sky tonight".

p.70 BEATRICE

Beatrice Chase (Olive Catherine Parr), 1874-1955, writer, especially of books on Dartmoor. Her most famous book, *The Heart of the Moor*, was written in 1914. In 1901, Beatrice added a window in the special writing-corner of her cottage at Widecombe-in-the-Moor; it was to become a well-known local landmark where visitors could see the writer at her desk inside; two titles reflect this: *Through a Dartmoor Window* and *The Dartmoor Window Again*.

p.71 RHYS AND PLATH

Rhys completed *Wide Sargasso Sea* whilst living in Cheriton Fitzpaine; Plath worked on *Ariel* in North Tawton.

p.75 FABULOUS BEE

H.D., American poet/writer 1886-1961, frequently stayed in the South-West and worked on some of her most significant texts whilst in the region.

p.77 CHERVIL

Temulentum, the species name of the plant Chervil, from Latin "intoxication", or "vertigo".

p.79 UNFINISHED BUSINESS

Quotes from Chrissy's poem, 'living wanting to live', and Tony's poem, 'Writing wanting to write', are embedded in the text.

www.ingramcontent.com/pod-product-compliance
Lightning Source LLC
Chambersburg PA
CBHW030048100426
42734CB00037B/584